Famous People

GUY FAWKES

1570 ~ 1606

Christine Moorcroft

Magnus Magnusson

Christine Moorcroft is an educational consultant and an Ofsted inspector, who was a teacher in primary and special schools and a lecturer in education. She has written and edited several books on history and religion and on other subjects, including personal and social education, science and English.

Magnus Magnusson KBE, has written several books on history and archaeology, and translated many Icelandic sagas and modern Icelandic novels. He has presented major television programmes on history and archaeology, such as *Chronicle*, *The Archaeology of the Bible Lands* and *Living Legends*, as well as the long-running quiz series, *Mastermind*. He is currently chairman of Scottish Natural Heritage, the Government body which advises on environmental issues.

ACKNOWLEDGEMENTS

The authors thank the following for their help: John Clark, Hazel Forsyth and Judy Stevenson (Museum of London).

Picture credits
National Galleries of Scotland: page 15
National Portrait Gallery: page 16
The Stock Market: page 19 (bottom)
City of York: page 6 (house interior)
Tessa Bunney: pages 4 (both), 6 (house exterior), 8
Professor Hugh D Edmonson: page 11
The Bridgeman Art Library: page 9
Getty Images: 13, 14, 19 (top)
The National Trust: page 12
Historic Royal Palaces: page 18

Published by Channel Four Learning Limited
Castle House
75–76 Wells Street
London W1P 3RE

Written by Christine Moorcroft and Magnus Magnusson
Illustrated by Jeffrey Burn
Cover illustration by Jeffrey Burn
Designed by Blade Communications
Edited by Margot O'Keeffe
Printed by Alden Press
ISBN 1-8621-5355-8

For further information about Channel 4 Schools and details of published materials, contact
Channel 4 Schools
PO Box 100
Warwick CV34 6TZ
Tel: 01926 436444
Fax: 01926 436446

Contents

Guy Fawkes' England

When Guy Fawkes was growing up, the only church to which people were allowed to go was the Protestant Church of England. The Roman Catholic church had been banned. A lot of people wanted to be Catholic but they could be sent to prison for having rosary beads or Catholic prayer books.

The children could not be baptised as Catholics. They had to be baptised in Anglican churches. Catholics had to get married in Anglican churches and, when they died, they had to have a Protestant funeral.

GUY FAWKES
Hereabouts lived the parents of Guy Fawkes of Gunpowder Plot fame, who was baptized in St. Michael - le - Belfrey Church in 1570.

The Anglican church of St Michael-le-Belfrey in York where Guy Fawkes was baptised.

Catholic services like this mass were no longer allowed.

Catholic priests had been ordered out of the country. They were sent to prison if they were caught. Some were even killed.

So those Catholics who had large houses made secret places in them in which priests could hide. This was a dangerous thing to do because they could be sent to prison for helping priests. There were secret Catholic weddings and baptisms.

Did you know?

• Elizabeth was Queen of England. She followed the Church of England religion which her father, Henry VIII, had begun. Before that, most people in England had been Roman Catholics.

• The Church of England is sometimes called 'Anglican' or 'Protestant'.

Growing up in York

Guy Fawkes was born in York in April 1570. His father's name was Edward and his mother's name was Edith. Guy had two younger sisters, Anne and Elizabeth. An elder sister, also called Anne, had died when she was a baby.

Guy's family was not rich but they were not poor either. His father was a lawyer. When Guy's grandmother died she had left a lot of money and jewellery to her family and friends.

Above is 32-34 Stonegate, York, the site of the house where Guy Fawkes was born and lived until he was about eight.

The photograph on the left shows what the inside of a house would have looked like when Guy Fawkes was a boy.

Guy's mother had been brought up as a Roman Catholic before it was banned. His father was an Anglican.

When Guy was about eight years old, his father died. A few years later, his mother married again, this time to a man who had also been brought up as a Roman Catholic.

So, although Guy had been brought up as an Anglican, when his mother remarried he became a Catholic. They held secret Catholic services in their home.

A change of faith

Guy went to a grammar school in York. The pupils had go to the Anglican church at six o'clock every morning. There were other boys at his school who were also Catholic. Two of them were John and Christopher Wright. He did not realise it then, but Guy was to meet these two brothers again in the future.

When Guy left school he lived with his mother and step-father in Scotton for about three years.

Guy was not poor. When he was 21 years old, he inherited his father's property. Ten months later, he sold all his land for £29. This was a lot of money in those days.

These are the cottages in Scotton where Guy Fawkes lived with his mother and step-father.

Even though he had this money, Guy had to earn his living. He left Scotton in 1592 and found a job in Sussex, as a servant to the Viscount Montague, and then to his son Antony. This was a good job for a young man to have, in the home of a wealthy lord.

But Guy wanted to be able to be a Catholic without having to hide it. So he decided to go to the Netherlands, as a soldier. There he would be able to worship freely.

Viscount Montague's family.
Guy was their servant.

The Netherlands and Belgium were ruled by Spain.

Did you know?

- England was at war with Spain, which was a Catholic country.

- Spain had sent a fleet of galleons, 'The Armada', to attack England in 1558. The English had defeated the Armada.

Soldier of fortune

At first Guy was a soldier in the English army, using gunpowder to blow up the walls of some of the towns in the low countries held by Spain. Then, around 1597, he left the English army to join a Spanish regiment in which there were many English Catholics. One was its commander, Sir William Stanley.

Sir William Stanley saw that Guy Fawkes was a good soldier. He promoted him to 'ensign', in charge of a company of soldiers.

Stanley planned to make things better for Catholics in England. He asked Guy to be his assistant.

This map shows the plan for how the Spanish could invade England.

Huddington Court, in Worcestershire, was the home of Robert Wintour, elder brother of Thomas, a soldier in Guy's regiment. It has two hiding places.

Sir William Stanley, Guy Fawkes and another soldier named Thomas Wintour went to Spain in 1598 to ask King Phillip III to invade England! Their idea was for the Spanish to take Milford Haven on the Welsh coast. Troops would march through Wales to the English counties in which many rich Catholics lived. There, all the Catholics would get together to rebel against Queen Elizabeth.

But the three men did not know that there were peace talks going on between England and Spain. The King of Spain was polite to them, but he did not agree to their plan.

Did you know?

- *Many Catholics in the court of Queen Elizabeth did not want to fight. They wanted peace.*

- *Elizabeth herself, who was now nearly 70, also wanted peace.*

11

Conspirators

On 20 May 1604, Guy Fawkes went to a secret meeting at an inn in London with Robert Catesby, Robert Wintour, John Wright and Thomas Percy. They had decided that something must be done so that the Catholics could be free to follow their faith.

In a private room, the men swore an oath of secrecy on a prayer book. They planned to blow up the House of Lords on the opening day of Parliament in the following year when King James I would be there! After the meeting they took Holy Communion, a Catholic service, with a priest named Father Gerard.

Above is a photograph of Robert Catesby's home in Chastleton, Oxfordshire.

Robert Winter
Christopher Wright
John Wright
Thomas Percy
Guido Fawkes
Robert Catesby
Thomas Winter
Bates

CONCILIVM SEPTEM NOBILIVM ANGLORVM CONIVRANTIVM IN NECEM IACOBI ·I·
MAGNÆ BRITANNIÆ REGIS TOTIVSQ ANGLICI CONVOCATIPARLEMENTI·

This is a drawing of eight of the 13 men who planned to blow up the House of Lords. It was drawn at the time when it all happened.

In May 1604 the men found lodgings near Parliament House where Guy could stay. He was not known to anyone in London and so he changed his name to John Johnson. The others left London and did not come back until October.

Robert Catesby had bought about 36 barrels of gunpowder, saying that it was for the English army in the Low Countries. Another man, Robert Keyes, joined the group and he looked after the gunpowder at a house just across the River Thames from the Houses of Parliament.

Did you know?

- *Queen Elizabeth died in 1603. James VI of Scotland, the son of Mary, Queen of Scots, became James I of England as well.*

- *He had been brought up as a Protestant while his mother was in England but his wife, Anne of Denmark, was a Catholic.*

The Gunpowder Plot

The building where Guy Fawkes was staying had a store-room which went under the House of Lords. It was being used by a coal merchant. Guy and the other conspirators paid him to leave so that they could rent it. By this time, four more men had joined them: Thomas Bates, Thomas Wintour (brother of Robert), John Grant and Christopher Wright (brother of John).

A drawing of the store-room beneath the House of Lords.

Soon they began to bring the barrels of gunpowder in, rowing boats across the Thames from Lambeth. They hid them under piles of coal and wood in the store-room. Nobody would notice it because the room was full of bits of stone, wood and other rubbish.

Three more conspirators joined the group in September 1605. One was Ambrose Rookwood, from whom Catesby had bought the gunpowder. He had a large stable of horses which would be useful. The second was Francis Tresham, Catesby's cousin, and the third was Sir Everard Digby.

By this time rumours were spreading among Catholics about a plot to destroy the government.

This is a painting of King James VI of Scotland and I of England. Guy Fawkes and the other conspirators planned to blow up the House of Lords while the King was there.

Did you know?

- *Parliament had been due to open in February 1605, but there were fears of an outbreak of plague in London.*

- *The opening date was moved to 3 October, but by the end of July there was still plague in the city.*

- *It was decided to open Parliament on Tuesday 5 November.*

Discovery

By the end of October 1605, all the gunpowder was in place beneath the House of Lords. The barrels were covered with lumps of coal and bundles of wood. The plan was for Guy Fawkes to light the fuse and to escape by boat across the Thames.

Robert Cecil, the Earl of Salisbury, who was the King's chief minister, had heard that there was a plot against the King.

A portrait of Robert Cecil, the first Earl of Salisbury, who was the King's chief minister.

Then, on the evening of 25 October, Lord Mounteagle was enjoying a dinner party at his home when a messenger brought him an anonymous letter. The letter warned him not to go to the opening of Parliament. Lord Mounteagle sent the letter straight to the Earl of Salisbury.

On 2 November, the Earl of Salisbury told other lords about the letter. By this time many of the lords had heard about a plot against the King and Parliament. They decided that, on the day before Parliament opened, all the buildings of the Houses of Parliament should be searched.

At 3pm on 4 November, Lord Mounteagle and some others walked into the cellar. They found Guy Fawkes, and asked him about all the wood and coal there. He told them that the fuel belonged to Thomas Percy and that he was looking after it.

Did you know?

- *Guy Fawkes did not know about the letter to Lord Mounteagle.*

- *Robert Catesby had heard about the letter, but he did not think anyone suspected the Gunpowder Plot.*

- *On 1 November, Lord Salisbury told the King about the letter.*

17

Trial and punishment

During the night of 4 November, King James had the cellar of the House of Lords searched. Guy Fawkes was there, dressed for travel, in a cloak, hat and boots. When he was arrested he gave his name as 'John Johnson'. The other conspirators fled on horseback when they heard what had happened.

The Tower of London, where Guy Fawkes was tortured and imprisoned until his hanging.

Guy Fawkes was taken to the Tower of London where he was questioned. He admitted that he was going to blow up the House of Lords. He would not give his real name or the names of the other conspirators. The King gave the order to torture him to make him talk.

Guy Fawkes was tortured, first with manacles and then on the rack.

This drawing of Guy Fawkes about to be executed was done at the time.

On 7 November Guy Fawkes told his torturers his name and, the next day, the names of five of the other conspirators. Then he told them the names of the others.

Four of the conspirators were killed by the people who tried to capture them and one died in the Tower. The others, including Guy, were sentenced to death. Guy Fawkes was the last to be taken to the scaffold on 31 January 1606. He asked the King to forgive him, said a prayer and made the sign of the cross. Then he was hanged.

The Houses of Parliament as they look today.

Did you know?

- *Robert Catesby, Thomas Percy and the Wright brothers were shot dead by the High Sheriff of Warwickshire's men.*

- *The first 'Bonfire night' was held on 5 November 1605, the day after Guy Fawkes was arrested. Bonfires were lit in London to celebrate the saving of the King and Parliament.*

Time-lines

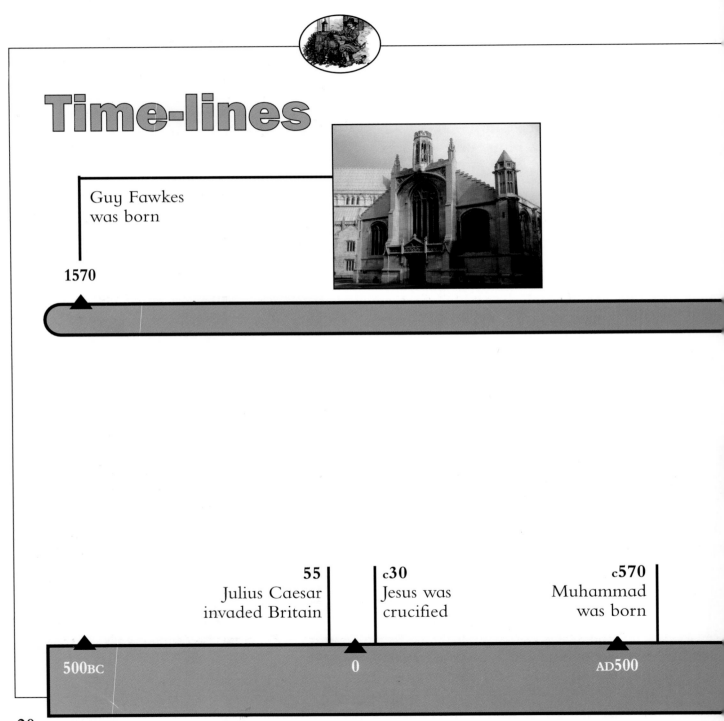

Guy Fawkes
was born

1570

55
Julius Caesar
invaded Britain

c30
Jesus was
crucified

c570
Muhammad
was born

500BC

0

AD500

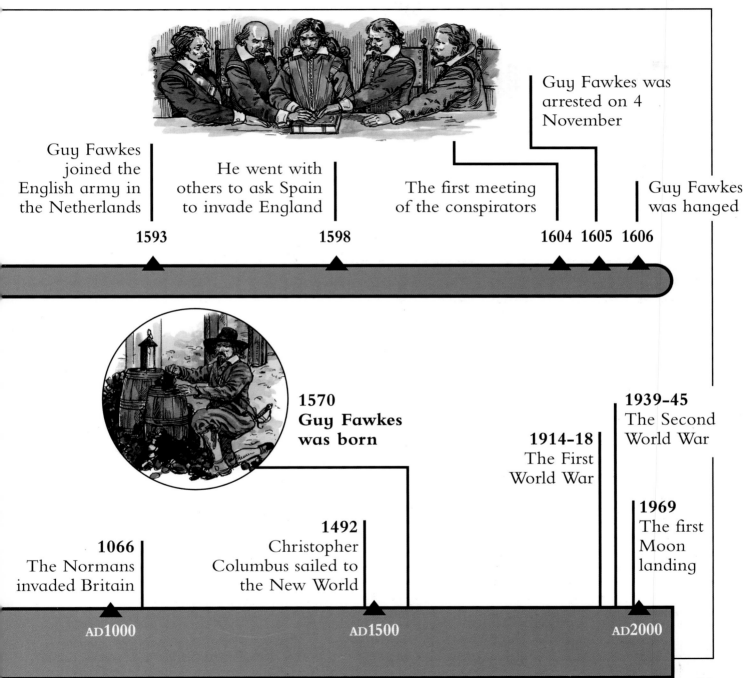

Guy Fawkes
joined the
English army in
the Netherlands

He went with
others to ask Spain
to invade England

Guy Fawkes was
arrested on 4
November

The first meeting
of the conspirators

Guy Fawkes
was hanged

1593

1598

1604 **1605** **1606**

1570
**Guy Fawkes
was born**

1939–45
The Second
World War

1914–18
The First
World War

1969
The first
Moon
landing

1066
The Normans
invaded Britain

1492
Christopher
Columbus sailed to
the New World

AD1000

AD1500

AD2000

How to find out more

More books to read

The Gunpowder Plot by Antonia Fraser (Mandarin, 1997)

History of Britain: The Stuarts by Andrew Langley (Heinemann, 1993)

The Gunpowder Plot by Rhoda Nottridge (Wayland, 1991)

Gunpowder, Treason and Plot by Lewis Winslock (Wayland, 1973)

The Gunpowder Treason by Henry Brinton and Patrick Moore (Lutterworth, 1970)

Places to visit or to which to write

Burghley House,
Stamford,
Lincs.
Tel 01780 52451

Geffrye Museum,
Kingsland Road,
London E2 8EA.
Tel 0171 739 9893.

Houses of Parliament,
London SW1A 0PW.
Tel 0171 219 3000.

Museum of London,
150 London Wall,
London EC2Y 5HN.
Tel 0171 600 3699.

Tower of London,
London EC3N 4AB.
Tel 0171 709 0765.

Glossary

Anglican *(4)* Another name for the Church of England faith.

baptise *(4)* To make people members of the Christian church at a special ceremony.

conspirator *(12)* Someone who takes part in a secret plot.

ensign *(10)* A soldier who led a company of soldiers during a war.

execute *(7)* To put to death someone found guilty of a crime.

galleon *(9)* A large sailing ship with cannons used in sea-battles.

grammar school *(8)* A school for the sons of 'gentlemen' (such as lawyers).

Holy Communion *(12)* A Christian ceremony.

inherit *(8)* To become the owner of property which was left to you by someone who died.

lawyer *(6)* Someone who works with the law.

Low Countries *(10)* In Guy Fawkes' time, the Netherlands and Belgium.

Today it includes Luxembourg.

manacles *(18)* Iron rings used for torture. The prisoner hung from them by his or her wrists.

mass *(5)* A Roman Catholic religious service.

minister *(16)* A person who leads church services.

oath *(12)* A promise which people swear they will keep. They usually hold a Bible or other holy book.

plague *(15)* The name given to a disease with no cure which killed many people.

rack *(18)* A wooden bed on which a prisoner was tortured by stretching.

regiment *(10)* A unit to which a soldier belongs.

rosary *(4)* A string of beads used by Roman Catholics to count prayers.

viscount *(9)* (pronounced vy-count) A nobleman.

Index